WHO PUT THAT THERE?

Written by Gina Nuttall
Illustrated by Amerigo Pinelli

Woody was late.

He should have been at football training by now.

He ran around like a bullet, looking for his football. But he could not find it.

Oops! Woody ran right into his mum.
She was crouched down, looking in the pushchair.

"OUCH! Slow down!" she said.

"Have you seen my football?" asked Woody.

"No," said his mum, very annoyed.
"Have you seen my brown handbag?
Help me look for my bag and
I'll help you look for your football."

"Good," agreed Woody.

But he forgot about slowing down.

He ran into the living room like a mad bull.

Oops! His sister Joy was standing by the bookshelf.

"OUCH! Slow down!" Joy howled.

"Have you seen my football and Mum's brown handbag?" asked Woody.

"No," said Joy, looking very put out.

"I've been looking for my cookbook," she said. "Help me look for it and I'll help you look for the football and handbag."

"Good," agreed Woody. "But I've got to hurry."

Woody found Joy's cookbook under the dirty towels.

Joy found Mum's handbag in the toy box.

All Mum found was the baby, coiled up asleep.

So where was Woody's football?

Suddenly there was a loud THUD in the hall.

Woody, Mum and Joy stopped looking. They ran into the hall.

"OUCH!" said Dad, bumping down the stairs.
"Who put that there?"
"Woody, Dad has found your football!" said Mum.